This Book Belongs to

SPACE

Doodle Kid
A B C

PEOPLE
WHO LOVE TO EAT
ARE ALWAYS
the
BEST
PEOPLE

LOVE
LOVE

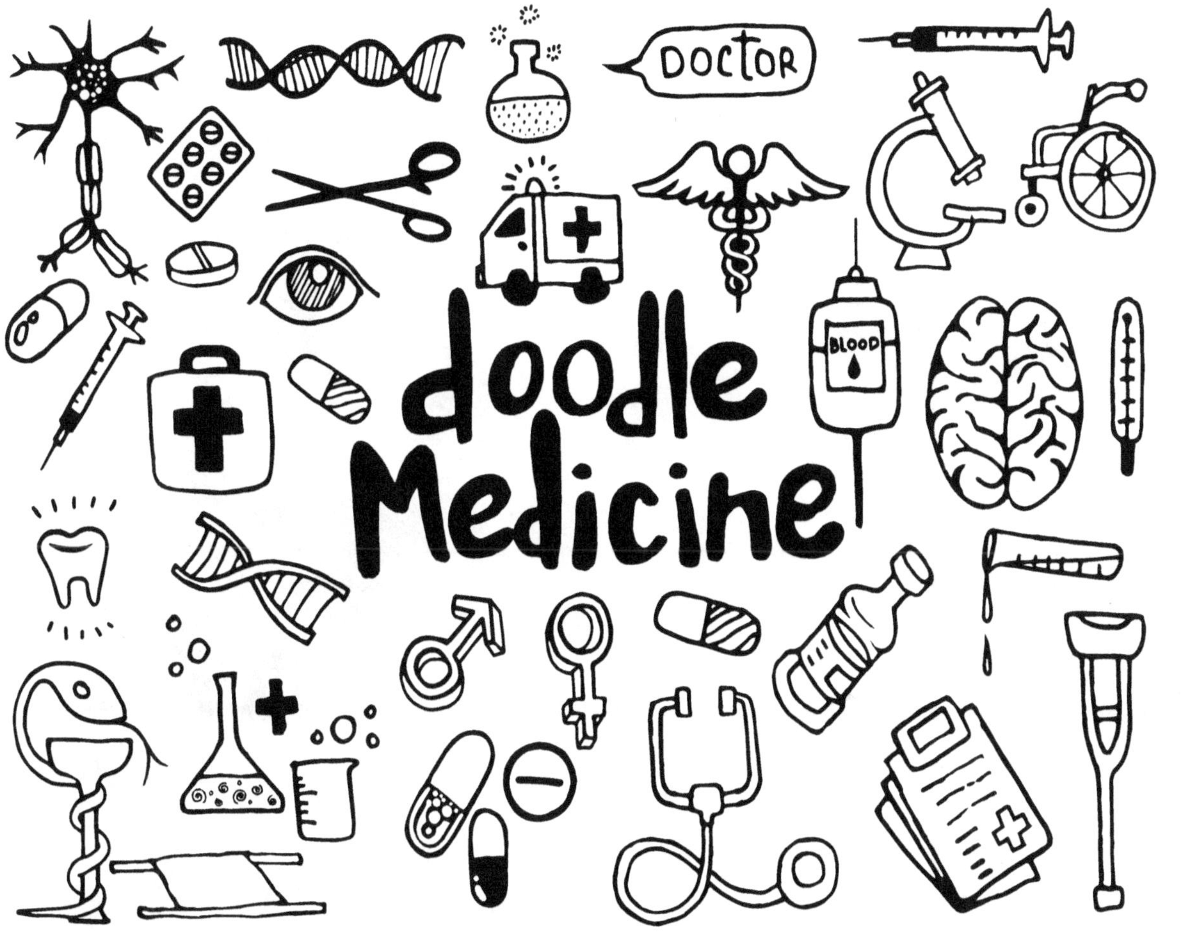
DOCTOR
BLOOD
doodle
Medicine

ALONE
WE CAN DO SO
LITTLE
TOGETHER
WE CAN DO SO
MUCH
TEAM WORK

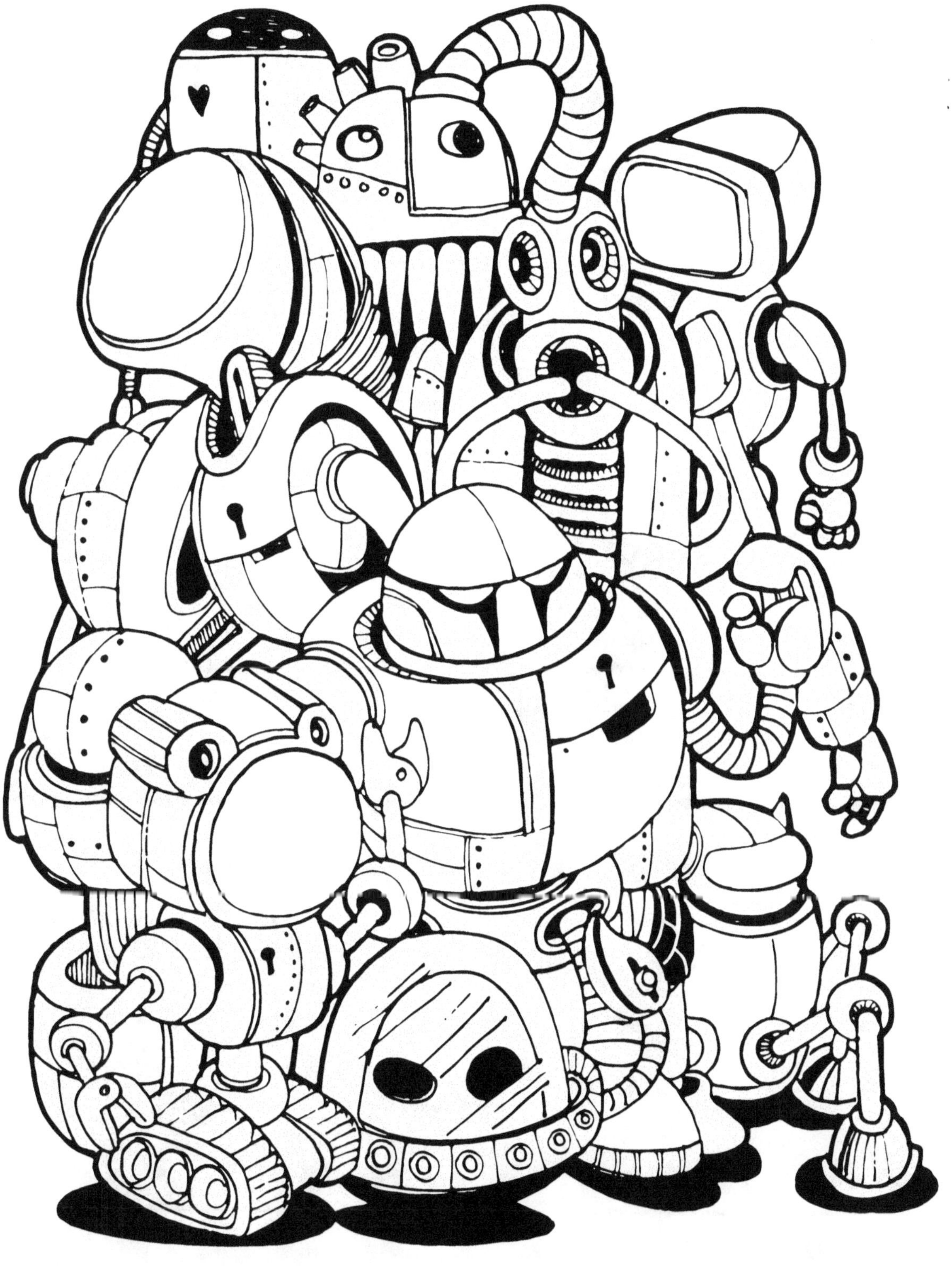

FAMILY
FRIEND
FOOD
FUN

HAVE FUN

SUCCESS
PLANNING
IDEA
SOLUTION
ACHIEVEMENT
CONCEPT
LEADERSHIP
BUSINESS
$

DON'T WISH
FOR A GOOD BODY
WORK FOR IT
TIME
for
FITNESS
STOP DREAMING
START DOING
SMALL STEP
BIG CHANGE

CAPTURE
the
GOOD TIME
SNAP
LIFE IS LIKE
A
CAMERA
Focus On What's
IMPORTANT

doodle
Party

Party

LOVE
LOVE

I HOPE YOUR
BIRTHDAY
IS FULL OF
SUNSHINE
and
RAINBOWS
and
LOVE
and
LAUGHTER

I ♥ MUSIC

Crazy
MONSTERS
funny
!

www.ingramcontent.com/pod-product-compliance
Lightning Source LLC
Chambersburg PA
CBHW080602060326
40689CB00021B/4910